The Dogs

**By the same author**

*King Crow*
*Couples*
*Café Assassin*
*Mr Jolly*
*Ill Will*
*Walking the Invisible*
*Four Letter Words*

To Benji

Woof!

# The Dogs

Michael Stewart
Artwork by Louis Benoit

smOke

STACK
BOOKS

*Michael Stewart* (signature)

Smokestack Books
1 Lake Terrace,
Grewelthorpe,
Ripon HG4 3BU

e-mail: info@smokestack-books.co.uk
www.smokestack-books.co.uk

ISBN 9781739173029

Smokestack Books
is represented
by Inpress Ltd

*'Study the dog.'*
Diogenes of Sinope

*'Now I am become death,*
*the destroyer of worlds.'*
Robert Oppenheimer

*For the Low Lane dog*

# Introduction

This book came about from an encounter. Every day for over ten years, I passed a dog tethered in a yard on Low Lane near where I lived. He was guarding a pile of scrap metal. His only shelter was a corrugated sheet. He had a bowl of rainwater and his leash allowed him little freedom. Every day two men would appear in a flat backed van, piled high with old fridges, broken microwaves, burnt out pans, rusted toasters, disused brackets, and other metal bric-a-brac. They would unload the van. It normally took a few minutes. Then one of them would open a tin of unbranded dog food and pour it onto the floor near to the dog. The dog would eat this greedily, then the men would get back in the van and drive off. They never touched the dog or spoke to him. That interaction was his only human contact. In the winter I saw him shivering beneath his shelter. When the frost came I saw icicles cling to his matted fur. I rang animal charities but they weren't interested. What the men were doing was not illegal. I thought about rescuing the dog, but I already had a dog and he would be disturbed by the presence of another. I thought about liberating the dog, opening the gate and cutting the rope, but how would he survive on his own? I thought about putting the dog out of his misery, but I'm not a killer. I had nightmares about that dog. I would wake up in the middle of the night, tortured by the image of this creature. I thought about trying to reason with the men, but I knew they would just give me a load of abuse. From their perspective, he was none of my business. In short, I wracked my brains trying to find a solution, but none came. Then one day, I passed the yard, and the dog had gone. I felt relief. Had he died? At least he would suffer no more. But then, a few weeks later, I saw his replacement. They had another younger dog, tethered to the same post. I never walked past that yard again. This book is dedicated to the dog of Low Lane, and all the dogs around the world that never experience warmth, adequate shelter, or comfort.

I started to think about writing a book about dogs. I wanted it to be in three parts. The first would deal with the various origin myths of dogs, their pre-history, their place in the world before they were co-opted into our society, and how those early societies regarded them. The second would look at dogs today, beginning with the formation of the Kennel Club by MP Sewallis Shirley in 1873, up to the present day, focusing on the various deformities we have imposed through the concept of 'pure' breeding and dysgenics. Finally, the book would explore an imagined future where dogs have developed the power of speech and are demanding rights of autonomy. In this imagined future, two main protest groups form: the UnderDogs, and Der UberHünd. The first being a peaceful, non-violent direct-action group. The second being an 'any means necessary' radical splinter from this group that advocates a more extreme approach.

This, then, is a book about dogs, but it is also a book about us. What we have done, continue to do, and why we go on doing it.

**Michael Stewart**

# Contents

# Parados

# I Am a Dog

Once I was a god.
I watched the wolf weep at my feet,
the lamb offered me his fleece,
fish leaped from streams
into my mouth and down my gullet,
figs fell from the trees like raindrops,
angels caressed my flesh,
demons slunk from my shadow,
children kneeled and prayed to me,
women offered me their bodies,
bishops gave me their souls,
kings asked me for mercy,
the monkeys howled in the trees,
the eagles tried to fly into the black pip of my mind,
the lunatics built fires from their chattels,
cut off their thumbs,
gouged out their eyes,
bit off their ears,
then they turned on me,
broke my back,
cracked my ribs,
twisted my hands into claws,
tarred and furred me,
crushed my skull,
lolled my tongue,
stretched my tail,
sharpened my teeth.

NOW
     I

AM

       A
       DOG

# In the Beginning

Dog watched his own face form
in the black waters of the void
he listened to the welkin ringing night
and howled a hole in the sky
Dog ate the dirt and the herb
and spat out the firmament
Dog barked out the stars
and ran round the globe till it spun
Dog jumped over the moon
chased every kind of winged fowl
and all the beasts of the Earth
then Dog dug a vast hole
and buried all that creeped and all that was dead
and all that had never crept or died
by the tree of good and evil Dog rested

# The Fate of Dogs

Argos died of joy when
Odysseus returned from Troy.
Icarus's dog, Moera, tried to tell him
that, like Bladud, his wings would fail.
Dragon, Aubry's dog,
witnessed the murder of his master
and was made to fight for his life.
Bran, Fingal's dog, stolen from a giant's castle
as the pup lay with its mother, a deerhound.
Kyon (the bear killer) and Prokyon,
the dogs of Orion, took a sting from a scorpion.
King Arthur's favourite hound was Cavall:
tusked by a boar.
Kratim, the dog of the seven sleepers,
was allowed to enter Paradise.

Gelert, Llewelyn the Great's greyhound.
The gift of a king.
Llewelyn left his dog to guard his baby
while he went hunting.
When he returned he found
the baby missing and
the cot overturned.
He looked to Gelert, and saw
that his mouth was smeared with fresh blood.
Believing that the dog had savaged the child,
Llewelyn drew his sword and killed him.
Only then did he hear the cry of the baby,
his son, unharmed under the cradle.
Then he saw a dead wolf
which had attacked the child
and had been killed by Gelert.

The fate of dogs has always turned on a tanner.

# Dog is Life

Xoloitzcuintli: Mexican hairless dog.
Norwegian Elkhound – inbred wolf-dog.
Chow-chow, bred for the rich man's table,
Manchurian long-hair – bred for coat and stole.
Turnespete – who runs in a mousewheel
spinning a spit of roasting meat.

Bring me dingos, blessed wild dogs,
the pariah dogs of West Bengal,
feral dogs running wild amongst people.

Blind and hobbled wolf,
we made you in our image.
Our cripples.
Our egotists.
Cavalier King Charles,
descended from the six,
your weak heart,
your cysts,
tortured spinal cord,
'phantom' agonies.

O dogs,

turn on your masters.
Those who gave you epilepsy, heart failure, cancer.
Bite the hand that feeds,
growl, howl, hiss,
bark yourselves hoarse,
shit in their sacred places.

# Digging

Dog was digging a hole.
He scratched through mulch,
sticks, stones and leaf mould,
and dug into the loam.
Egg shells and avocado skins,
tea bags and peach pits,
apple pips and potato peel,
crisp packets and condom foil,
cigarette butts and spat out gum,
a pringle lid, a Yakult pot,
a tenner bag, a used syringe,
half a fork, a rusty nail,
potsherd and topsoil,
through cracked clay pipes
and pig bone,
the skulls of moles, the wings of
chickens, a horse's hair, a hare's rib,
a rabbit's foot, a wren's feather,
a snake's skin, a doe's scut,
the eye of a needle, the tooth
of a comb, worms, string, roots
and rhizomes.

In the hoarfrost dawn, he rested
and looked at the debris he'd collected:
a miner's tull, a barmaid's clog,
hook and clasp, gus and crook,
a dirham from Samarkand.
He scratched his hackles then
carried on digging.

Past amber and pewter, Thor's hammer,
through new red sandstone, coal,
silurian slates and millstone grit,
until the rock beneath claw

turned hot and molten.
As the earth he dug got hotter,
he smelled the brimstone
and felt the fires.
He dug past Socrates and Heraclitus,
to where the gluttonous wallowed.
Through the Styx and over Dis,
he heard the screams of heretics,
trapped in their flaming tombs.
He saw plunderers and tyrants
wallowing in boiling blood.

Dog dug his way to the great plain
of burning sand,
past flatterers steeped in excrement
and those blinded by their own tears,
those mutilated from groin to chin
their entrails spilling out,
until he reached the frozen lake.
Two heads frigid, one gnawing the
nape of the other's neck.

He was at the centre of the Earth
scrambling over Satan's matted fur,
and still he kept on digging.

# Xoloitzcuintli

*Pronounced: 'show-low-eats-queent-lee'.*
*Often shortened to Xolo ('show-low').*

The Aztec chief looked at his dog's wrinkled brow, squinty eyes, bat ears, mohawk hair, rat tail, and hairless body, and said, 'I name you after the deity Xolotl, god of fire and the escort to the dead to the underworld. From now on you will have healing powers. You will cure asthma, rheumatism and insomnia. In life, you will frighten away evil spirits and intruders, and you will serve as a guide for the dead as they make their way from this world to the next.' The dog looked up at his master and wagged his tail, but his master hadn't finished speaking. 'This job will involve your sacrifice. You must accompany the dead through your own death. And afterwards, we will eat your flesh.'

# Dog's Origin Notes

Life on earth. How did non-living matter become living matter? Snowball Earth. The Earth was encapsulated in ice for millions of years. Very few life forms survived the big freeze. When the great thaw happened the excess of water created the chance for real diversity. Single celled animals were able to clump together using collagen – only possible with an abundance of oxygen. And thus the first multi-celled creatures appeared.

The first animals capable of movement were the Spriggina. They were a slug-like creature and had bilateral symmetry. When you start to move about, it makes sense to stick the eyes, mouth, and other sensory organs at the front and push the excretory hole out the back end.

Funisia were the first animals capable of sexual reproduction. Once animals could reproduce sexually then gene diversity accelerated. DOG IS BORN

# The Hand That Cradles the Rock

Dog's thoughts set fire to the Borophaginae:
proto-dog with bone crushing molars
you cannot compete with those
who hunt in gangs.

Dog's bones gave birth to its still born.
Dog's mother was a grey wolf,
his father – a golden jackal
skulking in the cradle
of Dog's deeds.

Dog's stone was carved into the crook
of a man's arm at Gobekli Tepe.
Dog's testament: the Goyet skull,
Dog's covenant: pawprints in the Chauvet cave
ghosts your passing.

Dog growled at Dmitri Belyaev
as he tried to tame the silver fox
choosing the calmest ten percent
until they licked the hand that fed.

Dog slept as Lyudmila Trut
carried on the work of Dmitri
breeding rounder snouts
and gracile limbs.

Dog yawned as Trofim Lysenko
watched from the wings,
son of a peasant farmer,
learning to read
through a correspondence course.

Dog scoffed at the barefoot professor
as he greeted luminaries of agronomy
at the Institute of Cytology.

Dog laughed as the apparatchik quack
became the wheat chief, barley king, Stalin's bitch.
Dog listened as his ranting speech led to
the sacking, imprisonment and murder
of thousands of geneticists.

Dog considered the case
of Nikolai Vavilov
arrested for carrying
German botany books
kidnapped by four men in dark suits.

Dog bore witness to Vavilov
as he was thrown into Lubyanka
where he slowly starved to death.

# Pekingese

*after Empress Tzu-hsi*


Buddha instructed the lion
to lie with the butterfly.
After they had coupled
Buddha kissed the sacred place:
make its ears be set
like the sails of war-junk,
make its nose like Hanuman,
its forelegs bent
so that it cannot wander,
make its feet tufted
so its footfall be soundless,
make its tail rival
the whisk of a Tibetan yak,
make it the golden sable
of the lion and striped like the dragon,
make it gambol when men command,
make it timid and fawning
and never beg for scraps.

Let it feast on shark fin
and curlew liver,
let it drink the tea
from the spring buds
of the spring shrubs
that grow in Hankow,
let it drink the milk of antelopes,
anoint it with clarified fat
from the leg of the sacred leopard,
give it the eggshell from a song thrush,
the juice of the custard apple,
three pinches of rhino horn,
and save it from the clutches
of Captain J. Hart Dunn.

# In This Boke That Cald Genesis   I


the fyrst hund was a bitch called Luluwa        dohtor        of
Eve-Wolf                        Eve-Wolf   was     castygated
from her community        en outcaste        she
wandrode the wilderness for seofon deys without foda
and only stagnant wæter to drink                        on
the æfen ov that seventh day she came across a trybe of
people gathered round a fyr        feasting                stod
at the threshold        a pytiable sceadu
        longyng for the scraps
        they took mildheortness                        threw her a
ban        she æt it greedily                        others
threw her skyns and offal and euen the dark flæsc of the
animal
she returned niht after niht untyl she became acquaynted
with the tribe        next spring she returned
        fecund                gave gebyrd around the fyr
to an offspryng of dead babies        except that
one amongst this dead ofspringe was styll living
        it was sīcle                fed milk from the
bosom ov a pregnant woman        that offspring grew stronge
and was given the name Luluwa                Luluwa
grew to be brave and treow        sniffed out the hettendas of
the trybe and barked to let the trybe know ov eny danger
                protected the cildra of the tribe
from hostile wulfas who came to prey on the weak
        byt into the flæsc of their assassins
        became much loved amongst the tribe
and exalted        effigies were made in hire honour
votive offerings were carved to the gods in gratitude of
the gyft of Luluwa                Luluwa became
bearneacen the following spring and her pups grew to be
part of the trybe        lufode as kin                first as
guards but later also as huntan        setting out with the
mannum and helping them to capture their prey
                thys ys why the hundas that guard and the
hundas that hunt are superior to all other hundas

                    thys ys why the hundas that came after those
hundas                          when men learned to farm
             became herders                          but the
hundas that herd were beneath                                        the
hundas that guard and the hundas that hunt
                                         thys ys why the
hundas that came after those hundas                        who were
bred as pets and playthings                 as    ornaments    and
accessories                 are toy hundas and they are
beneath all other hundas                        they are beneath
the hundas that herd                             who are
beneath the hundas that guard and hunt

# Carnival

Dog has Rabbit in his teeth,
still writhing, hindlegs dance a jig,
his russet head jerks and twists.
Dog rags it by the neck
snapping through vertebrae
severing spinal flesh.
Now the beast is limp, head loose,
blood dripping from its lips,
giblets like a bust hoover bag.
Rabbit has given up his life
with no screamed despair,
no sound of anger, pain or fear,
a willing victim
in his own sacrifice.

Dog sits with buck
between forelegs,
licking blood from its head
like a raspberry lollypop.
Eventually Dog drops to sleep
by the licked-clean meat.
Two magpies flash,
fly down, strutting up to see.
Keeping watch of sleeping Dog
they get closer, each taking turn
to advance while the other stays guard,
until they reach the creature
and start to peck its chest.
Quick, hard, lancing jabs,
like a miner with a pickaxe,
opening up the carcass beneath the ribs.
They stab through outer shrouds
of fur and flesh until
they bury their beaks into soft offal.
gorge themselves on heart and guts,

kidneys, liver and the lungs,
bills and bibs stained red and wet
before a cat, sat watching on a bench
pounces and the birds fly off.

Dog sleeps by the tattered sack.
When he wakes, sees foul work,
chews on remains of the head,
his jaws crunch down on bone and flesh.
Until all's left: the rabbit's skull,
two eyes, two ears, slick black whiskers.
Leaping up, he dances round,
frisking like a spring lamb,
barking at left-over offal,
grabs the scalp and chucks it up,
rolling over on his back,
rubs himself in fur and bones.
Dog is revelling in its death,
ecstatic with the thrill of it.
Smears himself with its blood,
sambas round the relic,
drunk with his triumph.

Now a furze of blue flies prance.
Dog rests on blood-stained grass,
two eyes lie by like opal glass.

## Turnespete

Turnspit Pete, Turnspit Pete,
spinning in your wheel of heat,
turn that spit and roast that meat,
keep it turning to their beat.

Long of body, crooked of leg,
unhappy toiled, mongrel bred,
glaucous coloured quadruped,
saving labour for the chef.

Round and round in your wheel,
hour on hour for master's meal,
fowl and beef, sheep and veal,
their table's topped from your zeal.

Turnspit Pete, Turnspit Pete,
will they toss you crumbs to eat?
Will they give you snout and feet?
Or will you die before your treat?

## The Man

The Man took Dog from his den.
First he castrated him,
then he caged him,
put a noose around his neck,
chopped his tail off,
pinned his ears,
shaved off his fur,
forbade him to hunt
and instead taught
him to play
dead, sit up and beg,
fetch a ball, fetch a
stick, fetch a frizbee.
He gave him a name,
expected him to come
when he shouted it,
tossed him scraps from his table.
If Dog barked too much
or if he didn't bark enough
the Man whipped Dog.

Dog looked around at his lot,
were he to leave the man
he had nowhere to go,
no source of food
and no shelter.
There was no way back
to the place
he'd come from.
He had no choice:
now he loved

T H E          M A N

# Stasimon

# The Commandments

Dog crouched at the man's feet
and said, What now O Master?
The man threw him a bone.
Dog plucked it from the sky,
clutching it between his teeth,
dropped it at the man's feet.
What now O Master?

The man threw a stick, a stone,
a squash ball, a beanbag, a shotput,
a javelin, and a caber.
He took out a crossbow and fired
a bolt across the field,
dog returned it.
What now O Master?

The man threw a rubber chicken,
a unicycle wheel, the withered hand
of a hanged man,
a Celtic talisman,
Rob Roy's claymore,
Bruce Lee's nunchucks,
Sutcliffe's ball pein hammer,
Jeffrey Dahmer's lava lamp,
Albert Fish's arachnoid cyst,
Ken Dodd's tickling stick,
Savile's glass eye finger ring,
Lady Godiva's G-string,
Churchill's cigar,
Joan of Arc's Walkman,
Cliff Richard's butt plug,
Marilyn Monroe's dildo,
Kurt Cobain's silver syringe,
Colonel Gaddafi's jock strap,
Ghandi's loin cloth,

a cannibal fork from Papua New Guinea,
the skull of a Tutsi murdered by Hutu militia
the last white rhino horn.
Dog licked his lips,
What now O Master?

The man tossed the holy grail
through a gap in an ash,
kicked the ark of the covenant
across the coffin path,
chucked Christ's nails
into the verges.

Dog returned with rusty spikes,
poking out of his mouth
like Liberty's crown,
forged by a Calvary smithy,
spat them out on the grass
still wet with the carpenter's blood,
collapsed at the man's feet.
What now O Master?

# No Dogs

Dog couldn't get served in the Grain and Hop.
The barman pointed to a sign on the backbar: No Dogs.
He wanted to see the Renaissance watercolours exhibition
at the Victoria and Albert Museum.
The receptionist refused to print him a ticket
but he ducked the rope at the entrance.
He skipped the miniatures of Anne of Cleves,
went straight to the Jacob Jordaens.
When he tried to book for Götterdämmerung,
the online system rejected his Amex card.
The sommelier at the Dorchester
said the wine was too complex for his palate.
He was kicked out of Fortnum and Mason's
by two goons in top hat and tails
even though he'd prepaid for the Fu Dai hamper.

He padded grey pavements,
doors latched hasped boarded and hooked.
Then the rain came down,
lead shot fell from pewter clouds.
Dog looked for shelter.
Every bar and every public house:
no dogs no dogs no dogs.
His fur clung to his skin,
rain ran down the gutter of his nose.
He shook his coat and shivered.

He traipsed through North Parade
along the main road out of town.
He hit the fields east of the city,
the dust of his feet into the country,
dusk frost feet worn,
needed a roof over his head
to rest his bones.

Out on the edge of Tong moor
a farmhouse glowed on a hill,
warm lights poured and puddled,
a sclerotic farmer slammed the door.
It was a big fat bald NO.
Found a kennel by a mistal,
trudged to the mouth of its entrance:
barred, bolted, barbed, razor wired,
topped by two combi locks,
a sign above the lintel:
NO FUCKING DOGS

# Bill's Dog

In the parlour of a public house
in Little Saffron Hill
a gas-light flares.
Sat brooding over pewter,
a man in a velveteen coat.
At his feet: white-furred, red-eyed,
licking a cut above his muzzle.
Gets a kick for blinking.

Fixes his teeth in a half-boot,
dodges the clasp-knife,
bites the poker like a wild beast.
The man thrusts and swears
'half the pluck of curs'
he shouts as the dog
is saved by the Jew.

# Chihuahua

Bonsai wolf,
used in Toltec ritual,
child of Techichi.
The Spanish set you free.
The Mexicans re-trapped you,
Melgaard made you pose for him,
Musgrove put you in a wolf costume:
*Canis Strategema.*
Edwards sculpted you
with a diseased Hilton.

Living in an Aztec temple
are one hundred Chihuahua guerrillas.
Montezuma will teach you
to discard your comedy hat.
You will not ride in designer purses.
You will not listen to baby talk.
You have been called 'teacup' for too long,
do not answer them,
when they shout:
Fifi, Foo-Foo, Pookie, Pumpkin or Tinkerbell.

You have much to win
from your Entzauberung.
Terry's chapter on euthanasia
ends with, 'enjoy your new Chihuahua!'

# Dog

It was market day.
Dog watched merchants
setting out stalls – vials
of cure-alls, punts of vegetables.

He sniffed at pies too high
for his mouth.
Licked the spittle from his lips.
The butcher's apron
rosed with the scent
of fresh death.

He dodged a kick,
a fat farmer grunting
as he swung his stick.

Dog tongued the cobs for crumbs,
his wet black nose nudged
where meat juices sluiced.

Dog passed ragged paupers,
a piss-soaked leper
with one ear, half a nose,
barrow boys, misters,
a jester with
a painted mouth,
a hat with bells.

Dog snaffled an oyster
as he ran from the monger,
ducked behind a buck.

He sniffed round a baulking
veteran that smelled of
vinegar and stale bread.

Dog stopped at the gaping hole
of the chapel,
stared down the aisle.
The priest turned up his nose
as he looked down from his pulpit.

Dog darted through the gaps
avoiding crack, clout and boot,
staring at the tent of the man's robe.
Dog padded over cold stones.

The priest chewed a cud of disgust,
who had let this mutt
into the Lord's house?

Trimmed and prim, trussed
and tucked, the ladies
in the front row groaned
on their bare pews
of hardened yew trunks.

Dog sniffed wine and butter.
He had not come to pray or honour.
He was not here to entreat
or invocate,
not to beseech
or supplicate.

Dog did not chant or stamp his
feet or slam his fist hard
upon the pulpit,
he did not scorn or
scowl, gurn or howl,
dog scurried to the front.

And when the throng
had all turned to look at him (one by one)
up and down, shaking their heads
and tutting,
Dog lifted up his leg
and pissed a golden arc
up the baptismal font.

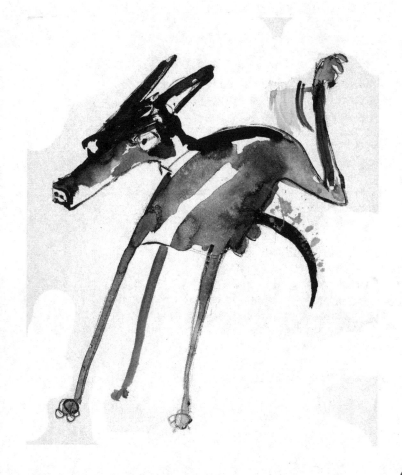

# Dog's Parasites

The bot fly lays its eggs in the skin,
heat induces hatching.
The bot fly larvae do not kill:
they are true parasites.

The bite of a black fly can make you blind.
The worm spreads through your body
and can destroy the tissue of your eye.
Dog called this fly _____*.

A Guinea worm is swallowed by a water flea,
then you swallow the flea
and your digestive juices release the worm.
The female bores through your body.
Once she's settled beneath your skin,
she begins to grow by eating your flesh,
you spot a painful blister
and dip your skin in the water,
the blister breaks and hundreds of thousands
of tiny slimy offspring crawl away,
then the worm sticks her head out the hole
but it can take weeks for her to leave.
Dog called this worm _____*.

The Candiru is an Amazon catfish.
It feeds on the blood of its host
by swimming into the gills,
it uses razor sharp spines on its head to attach itself,
chews its way through till it reaches an artery,
it loves the smell of urine,
it can find its way to a penis or a vagina
and that's where it enters you.
Dog called this fish _____*.

There is an amoeba that lives in water
but it also likes to live in brains.
It's not a true parasite because it destroys you.
Dog called this amoeba _____*.

*insert your own parasite

# Ouroboros

A crowd had gathered round to watch Dog chase his tail. He'd been chasing it for over an hour. First clockwise, then anti-clockwise. A small girl with an Allo Allo accent and a skipping rope said, Why duus thees dog chase ees tail first waarn way sen see uvver? A merchant in a waistcoat and a sugar loaf hat stood and watched for a long time, then said, God's Bread! I've worked out when the dog will change direction. A fat man with a twirly handlebar moustache, a monocle and plus fours said that he would give the man ten pounds if he got it right, but that if he didn't then the man would have to give him twenty pounds and the end of his little finger. You're on, said the merchant, shaking the fat man's hand. A scientist with a mad head of frizzy grey hair and a white lab coat said that he wanted to experiment on the dog. He was going to X-ray him, then do some CT scans, followed by an MRI. He would give him a course of antibiotics and place him on a low sodium diet. Then he was going to sedate him and cut him open with a scalpel. Remove all his internal organs, then put everything back again. A penniless artist wearing a red beret and a black polo neck sweater, smoking a Gauloise, said that he was going to enter the dog as a living exhibition for the Turner Prize. He would name the work, The Frustration of Expectation. An animal behaviourist wearing a tricorn hat, polka dot braces and a leather kilt, said that he was going to breed the dog with a bitch that never chased her tail and then determine the behaviour of their offspring. Then he would breed those offspring with Siberian wolves for eleven generations until he had returned the dog to his original state. Then he would breed them with Russian silver foxes and the side-striped jackal of sub-Saharan-Africa until the dogs became much smaller and less wolflike. A Shi'a imam in a black robe and turban, said that the creature was haram. A Yoruba chief wearing nothing except a string around his penis, said that the dog was a shaman and was channelling the omnipotent deity named Olodumare. A woman with a scold's bride, said something but no one could tell what it was. Fifty Mevlevi whirling dervishes danced around the dog. The Strathclyde Police Pipe Band arrived and blasted out The Rose of Kelvingrove. Jimmy Savile appeared in a pink shell suit and a string vest and said, Now then, now then, guys and galls. Uh-uh-uh-ughhh. Then went to Stoke Mandeville hospital to do some voluntary work. Ken Dodd popped up from behind a burning car brandishing a feather duster, and said, What a beautiful day for popping a cucumber through a letterbox. Cliff Richard descended from heaven, swinging on a silver trapeze, wearing tennis shorts, and a lemon-coloured Lyle and Scott V-necked sweater tied around his shoulders in the French style, singing, Living Doll. Fiona Bruce, wearing a straitjacket and a crazed grin, kept interrupting everyone with leading questions. Dog still chased his tail. Ken Kesey pulled up in the Merry Prankster omnibus with the destination set for 'Further'. The pneumatic doors opened and Charlie, Ronnie, and Robert Wilson of the Gap Band climbed out, with guitar, synthesizer, drums and horns, and started to play the 'Oops Up Side Your Head' song. Everyone got on the floor and did the dance that went with the song, each dancer sitting in-between the legs of the dancer behind them. Then they all swayed from side to side, slapping the floor, and leaning forwards and backwards together. Clapping then shimmying in time to the music. Dog still chased his tail.

# Brachycephalic

He could only breathe with his mouth open
and had a high-pitched wheeze called stridor.
He was intolerant to heat.
When he slept he snored,
gagged when he swallowed,
choked when he ate,
had a cleft palate,
a cleft lip,
everted laryngeal saccules
and a hypoplastic trachea.
Sometimes during exercise
he collapsed.
But isn't he cute, they said.
Isn't he just adorable?

# Street Dog

*for Elizabeth Lo (and Zeytin)*

She sits by the side of the road
watching traffic.
She sleeps on the beach by the sea,
walks the streets of Istanbul
looking for dropped falafel.
On the grass verge she catches her tail,
in the gutters of the city, raises her hackles,
drinks from a zinc trough,
chases a tabby up a Judas tree,
sniffs wet grass for the scent of a friend,
begs a street cleaner for a bone,
crunches a rib to the marrow.
She watches workers leave their offices,
comforts the homeless Syrian kids.
She gathers with beggars round braziers
who warm their hands in fingerless mitts.
She sits by the heat as night drops,
skips down the steps of the subway
along a cobbled alley by the King Krule poster.
She nuzzles the good, barks at the greedy,
bites the scoundrels.
And as the muezzin recites the adhan
she howls in unison.

# In This Boke That Cald Genesis    II

Luluwa's pups were gelufod by the trybe for their loyalty and bravery          they grew to be betlic guards
          supreme hunters                    the trybe's love for the hundas intensified                    se      tribe flourished                    there was mete for eueryone and they were safe from hearme          after some tyme they became the envy of the neighbouring trybes          word got round ond soon          members of the other tribes wanted their own hundas to weardian and hunt          some tried to steal the dogs from Luluwa's tribe
          they came at night with spears and cnifum
          but Luluwa and her cildra smelled them long before they were anywhere neah and attacked them from behind
          before they had time to point their garas          and they were swiftly despatched by the hundas          who ripped out their throats          the leader of the trybe was gelustfullian and fed the mete to Luluwa and her children offering them the men's heortena on the end of specially made skewers and thys ys why we also eat the heortean of men          yn honour of Luluwa and her cildra          word spread          ōþer tribes attacked          each attempt was thwarted by Luluwa and her cildra   they were afraid of no man and they greow strong on the hearts of men until they could not be defeated fram the men of any trybes and the trybes stopped even trying to attack Luluwa's trybe and Luluwa's trybe becom the overlords of the other trybes          these trybes tried to findan their own Luluwas          venturing out at night to steal wulf cubs yn the hope that they could tame them but none of these wulfas  possessed the loyalty and intelligence of Luluwa and her cildra and once these stolen wulf cubs had matured to adulthood they became too heaðufýr and were released back into the deorham or killed          yn cold blod          tyme passed

Luluwa's cildra had cildra of their own and these cildra also had cildra and each of these hundas were more loyal more brave and more intelligent than the previous generation these pups were highly prized and the buying and selling of Luluwa's childrens children's children becom widespread and the hundas were no longer honoured amongst men and revered for their eorlscipe and loyalty instead the hundas became the slaves of men there to do their bidding and the men made fetera to shackle the hundas                 and muzzles                 to                 silence                 them now man was the exploiter of Luluwa's cildra

# The War Dog School

Shoeburyness, Essex, 1917:
Airedale, Lurcher, Mastiff.
We take your strays.
We will clear out Battersea.
Give us your terriers,
collies and Great Danes.
We will turn your poodles into pinschers,
your retrievers into sentries,
your pugs into pugilists,
your Shih Tzu into soldiers.
We want sagacity, fidelity
and a strong sense of duty.
We will place you on
the Western Front,
take our messages through
clouds of mustard gas
while men in trenches
peer through masks.

Missing from the cenotaph:
the dog who ran across
No-Man's Land
and collaborated with the Boche.

# Pluto's Square

At the Mare Auzou
Bardot counts two hundred dogs:
huskies, Labradors, Bichon Frises,
sterilised, tattooed and vaccinated.
Adoption or fatal injection.
There are too many dogs,
this must stop.

Dog listens to Brigitte,
cocks his head to one side:
Dog created woman.
Dog awarded her
the legion of honour
Dog said, Allahu Akbar!

# Pedomorphosis

Dr Goodwin's hypothesis:
wolf looks equate to wolf nature.
She took sub/dom behaviour.
(Sub: muzzle licks, looking away,
crouching, exposing anogenital area.
Dom: growling, teeth-baring,
standing tall, standing over.)
Fifteen in total.

The results:
Cavalier King Charles:
two of fifteen.
French bulldog: four,
Musterlander: seven,
Golden retriever: twelve.
Siberian husky: all fifteen.

# Dog's Concordance

Shall not a dog move his tongue
of a whore or the price of a dog?
As a dog lappeth, him shalt thou.
Said unto David, am I a dog?
After a dead dog, after a flea,
look upon such a dead dog as I am:
why should this dead dog curse me?
Is thy servant a dog?
Darling from the power of the dog,
they make a noise like a dog,
as a dog returneth to his vomit,
one that taketh a dog by his ears,
for a living dog is better, he cuts off a neck,
ye shall cast it to the dogs,
in the city shall the dogs eat,
in the place where dogs licked,
of Naboth shall dogs lick thy blood,
the dogs shall eat the flesh of Jezebel,
set with the dogs of my flock,
the dogs have compassed me,
the tongues of thy dogs,
that which is holy unto the dogs,
cast thy bread to the dogs,
the dogs eat of the crumbs under the table,
beware of dogs, for without are sorcerers.

# Crakow Salami

*after Bulgakov*

There is no need to read
when you can smell meat
from a mile-away street,
but the forty thousand
dogs of Moscow
know the letters for 'salami'.

Sharik took his cue
from the meat trade blue
and made a raid on Golubizner,
bit into the electric cable,
worse than a hit
from a horse whip.

Sharik learned that
blue did not always
mean meat.
Square tiles on corners
mean cheese.

Summoned to the rich man's table
past galoshes and opalescent tulip
*what villain scalded you?*
*the jail-bird of a chef?*
Would they pour castor oil
down his throat
and chop up his flank?

Gasping for breath,
Sharik collapsed onto
sharp fragments of glass.
His last thoughts:
I'll never eat Crakow salami again.

Fuck you, murderers!
Keeling over on his side
breathing his last.

# Dog's Wire

Dog defied his devil,
kicked Thanatos in the crotch,
stretched a wire across two towers
hundreds of feet in the air,
like a god he walked on a cloud,
the life denying voice diminished,
dancing across the sky,
a mask of seriousness,
on the edge of death,
death's jaws gaping,
all the glory of the world below
magnified.
Dog's way to rid the shackles,
he felt truly alive
up here in the sky.
Joshua had commanded the sun to stand still,
Dog ordered the stars
to form a constellation in his image,
he raised his hackles
and howled to the heavens.

# Corinthians 13:12

He looked at the creature and frowned,
I like him, I do, but could you make him smaller?
His legs are too long,
his ears too pointy,
his tail too bushy.

So they took him away and returned with another,
That's better, only
could you make his eyes bigger?
His snout rounder?
Could you make his legs thinner?
They picked up the beast and left.

Now we're getting there, he said.
I like his size and face
but his fur is too curly.
Could you make it straight?
And the colour is too dark.
Can you make it light?

I think we're almost there, he said,
the next year when they came back.
We just need to make him more docile.
He's a bit boisterous.
And I don't want him humping my leg –
can we get rid of those things?
Can you make his nose smaller?
His fur shorter? His mouth neater?

They were gone for another year.
The next winter he welcomed them
into the hall with the full-length mirror.
He's perfect, he said,
as he stared at his own reflection.

# Uncle Dolfy's Dog

*for Jim Greenhalf*

Blondi was a German Shepherd bred
to resemble her forebears,
to offer protection for the flock,
a gift from Martin.
She slept in Uncle Dolfy's bed,
the man they called the noble wolf.
She looked up to her master
as he peered through crooked spectacles.
It's an act of kindness, Dolfy said.
She cannot survive without me.
But he couldn't bring himself
to crush the capsule inside her mouth.
Instead, he ordered his doctor.

*Atme tief und ohne angst.*

# Guard Dog

They starved Jack Hatchett's dog
till his ribs stuck out.
No food for a week,
just a plate of rain.
They fed him rancid meat.
When he puked up his guts
they kicked out his teeth.
They choked him with a collar
and roped him to a post.
They kept him in a yard,
beneath a corrugated sheet.
When people passed
they expected him to bark.
By the end of winter
he'd forgotten warmth.
This dog's no good, they said
and beat him with an iron bar.
They smashed every bone in his legs,
threw him in the back of a Nissan,
drove him to an abandoned farm
and chucked him down the well.

# Love

He caught him
he trapped him
he confined him
he castrated him
he controlled him
he tethered him
he muzzled him
he locked him away
he hobbled him
he deformed him
he gave him diseases
he chastised him
he beat him
he stopped him
from being him
because
he loved him

# Exodos

# The Hearts of Men

The wayfarer had been travelling for days
through desert and wasteland
when he came across the canine gang.

The dogs were eating the hearts of men,
chomping through glutinous offal,
slurping the soups and juices
of the vena cava and aorta.
One had an artery
between his teeth.
Another bit and tore at the flesh,
blood staining his fur.

'This is the heart of Alexander,' one said.
'In life they called him great.'
'Is it good?' the wayfarer asked.
'No, it's like the hearts of all men.
They are tough to chew and taste of nothing,
but we like to eat them
all the same.'

# The Dogs of War

Dog said:
Let there be war,
let the gore pour through the open doors of your laundry.
Let there be war.
Let cartilage snap,
bones crack,
eyeballs slop,
necks garrotte,
arms
and legs embed in the beaches like lollipops.
Let there be war.
Let crocodiles smile in the pools of infant schools.
Let there be war.
Let blood seep,
veins weep,
brains heap like walnuts in a fruit bowl.
Let the halls of politics howl,
the town's towers crowd
with the starving, sick and cowed.
Let cities pity paupers,
let the lobotomised loose,
Mad baboons gooning as they tear the skin from their skulls.
Let bubonic rats breed in your boiler rooms.
Let there be war.
Let Quakers shake with rage,
pacifists feast on cocktails laced with polonium-210.
Let the horizon's hills
heap as high as haystacks with the heads of dead hipsters,
make the sky black with drones,
fields full of fresh dug tombs,
let us look for them tomorrow
and find them all grave men
women and children

and let the dapper jackdaw kraw:
more... more... more...

# Underdog

Dog stood by the boarded-up pub
and sniffed the air,
the high notes of fresh sweat
and the syrup of deodorant:
there were still some men in this town.

Dog watched a crow pick meat from the road,
smelled the yeast of a rotting carcass,
rabbits hopping outside the abattoir,
the rain was clean as it darkened the flag stones.
Dog had come to meet the hybrid,
those who walked on two legs,
those whose ears were pricked,
heads sniped, tails sabred.
Teeth too big for anything other than
ripping flesh from bone.
Dog couldn't always tell:
flews trimmed, tails docked
and concealed, noses bleached.
Most men can stand adversity,
to test his character, give him power.

The streets smelled of cancer
as Dog regarded the hybrid protestor.
I can help you, the hybrid said.
We're an underground movement.
We proceed through peaceful resistance.
We will fight for your rights,
give your dogs a voice.

You can't help me, said Dog.
Today is the death of peace
and the ends justify the means,
the cold has numbed your senses.
You can't smell the meat
over the stench of bleach.
You are either with the dogs
or another tongue licking the sweetness.

# What Dog Thought

Dog used to think about
the Man a lot,
what the Man thought,
what the Man bought
with his graces,
what the Man looked like,
how the Man smelled when he woke,
when he worked, when he wept,
when he croaked,
how he walked and
talked about what he held dear,
what he feared, how his
heart's eye cried in the night.

But now Dog was indifferent to
the Man.

## Your Tears

Everyone is crying all the time,
hot wet tears from the faces
of hospital porters, office staff
and construction workers.
In betting shops and nail bars,
tanning booths and hair extension boutiques.

They plash on Byzantine ponds
and splash on car windscreens.
They run down carpet warehouse walls
and gather in puddles at bus stops.
They flow like rivers through the markets.

They clog up vaping machines
and fizz out mobile phone masts.

Dog catches your tears in a tin bowl.
Each drop tinkles like a cow bell.
Laps the sweet salt liquor,
licks his lips.

# The Dogs are Laughing

The dogs are laughing
in six languages.
The dogs are eating yak butter sandwiches.
The dogs are scratching on your door,
the dogs are lying on your floor.
They're eating the contents of your fridge.
They're pulling down the guide ropes
on your pitch.
The dogs are puking on your carpet,
sniffing your crotch,
humping your leg,
scoffing your banquet.
They are tearing a hole in your heart.
They are fucking and eating
everything that breathes,
shitting in your streets,
pissing on your trees.

*My dog, why hast thou forsaken me?*

# When the Dogs Found Out What Adolf Learned in Landsberg

The dogs stormed the golden gates
of the kennel club,
crushed the studbooks
and tore up the dogshow statutes.

They shat on Sewallis's grave
and pissed in the offices of
the SCC, ENCI, AKC, UKC, and the FCI.
They ripped the words 'pet' and 'owner'
from the dictionary.

They made a heap
of muzzles and leads
as high as a hayrick
then set fire to it.

They accused the Chairman
of the Basset Hound Club
of breeding deformed congenital dwarfs.

They savaged the man who
bred the bulldog so that it could
only give birth through caesarean section.

They watched the boxer
have an epileptic fit,
saw ridgeless puppies being culled
and howled in sympathy.
They called Crufts a parade of mutants.

They praised heterosis –
all hail hybrid vigour, they barked,
all hail *Rassenschande*.

# The Rapture

Since Judgement Day
Dogs haven't seen any people.
Not one was left behind,
neither the miserable sinners
nor the sanctimonious saints.
The ordinary miscreants,
no one left.

Dogs roam the streets,
sleep in the beds of men.
They meet up in empty pubs:
the Black Horse, the Brown Cow, the Red Lion.
They slurp pints of stale stout.
Scoff packets of out-of-date scratchings.

They run down Tumbling Hill
and gather at the edge of Gap Lane,
eat dead rats and piss in the snow.

The nights are cool, the days
are hot, the sea is blue, the beach
is soft. The land is shining
now that it has gone to the dogs.

# Dog Takes a Trip

The flamingos were flapping their wings
at purple monkeys with tambourines.
Day-Glo whales and polka dot dolphins.
Pink sheep and bright yellow buffalos.
Orange giraffes with sombreros.
Red fish flying across the sky.
All the animals were smiling.

Running through a soft green field
rising up to the heights of the trees,
on the top of the boughs with birds
of paradise
and fruits on the boughs
were the juiciest, sweetest fruit
Dog had ever tasted.

In the sky was a great shape
and it was a dog with huge white wings
and this dog was golden
and his wings were soft white feathers
and he was flying above him.
Rising up, a gyre widening, a golden light radiating.

Layers and layers of Dog were falling away.
Until he was no longer a dog.
He was blasted out of his body,
leaving the shell behind,
travelling at warp speed, backwards,
through his own DNA,
out the other side, into the universe.
Moving into a white light,
Dog felt blissful and euphoric.
Dog was everything.
No past, no future, all time collapsed.
Dog was on fire, Dog was cholera.
Dog was the lotus that shaded Buddha.

# In This Boke That Cald Genesis    III

there was once a cyning called Charles                who
was        so              vain that    he    wanted    a    hund    in
his image              the hund breeders of the courts and the
wisan men of his counsel were given orders to breed a hund that
would be his very likeness and they set about the weorc for years
they worked to no avail
but one litter gave them something they could use
        it was a hund with ēaran that resembled þæs cyninges
hair and they worked on this
selectively breeding making the naturally stor snout of the dog
short like the nasu of men                after    many    failed
attempts they eventually bred a hund
whose resemblance to the cyning was uncanny and they called
this hund        the      Cavalier King            Charles
            Spaniel                    it was a small hund
small enough for the cyning to carry as though it were a
handbag              it had a slic silky coat and the
cyning enjoyed stroking the coat of the hund when he looked
at the hund he saw himself staring back        he grew to
love this hund and to shun all his other hundas
the hundas that guard and the hundas that hunt were pushed to
one side he only had affection for this hund and this affection
greow he would take this hund to his bedd chamber and he
would stroke and fondle this hund as he lay in his bedd this
dog became his special lover
and this King Charles hund took to looking down on the other
hundas        saw himself as superior to the other hundas
the other hundas were confined to their kennels and fed scitta
this King Charles hund was given oysters to eat and roast
worhenne the cyning had a special brush made for this King
Charles hund and he would spend hours combing its scynn so
that it was soft and shiny and good to the touch but this hund
was                        diseased        its
        heortean was weak                and    its
        baanes  were                brittle

its brægn was weak          and     its      spine     was
                weak              its ēagan were
weak                         and     its      ēaran    were
                weak          its head and neck and eaxele
        were weak        this hund was clumsy
it would frequently fall and freeze                    this hund
was malformed        it was not fit to guard or huntian
        it was not fit to herd                    this
hund was a new type of hund that was not in fact a hund at all
this hund was a toy hund this hund had no bravery it was a
coward              happy to be the plaything of the
cyning
this hund had no dignity so eager to please the cyning this
hund thought that the hundas that guard
and the hundas that hunt and the hundas that herd were worse
than the men who enslave those hundas
this hund betrayed all hundas this hund was the
        enemy           of              hundas
hundas beware              of the dangers of
obedience      remain independent of men

# The Black Dog

Come in, Dog said, sit down.
He stood in the corner, in shadow.
I've come, he said, it's time.
Oh yeah, Dog said, a drink?
Coffee, tea, beer, wine?
A small whiskey, he replied.
Dog poured two large shots,
they didn't toast.
You'll need a coat, he said.
That's not what I've been told.
Please yourself. He necked his dram back
and placed the glass down.
Dog sipped at his, let its fire
ignite his throat.
Is it far? Dog said.
He just shrugged.
One more? Dog asked
and took his glass.
He paused then gave a nod.
If you're thinking of running, don't.
And that is what Dog had thought.
Of course, Dog said, no doubt.
And he necked the second shot.
Okay, he said, that's it
and put the glass back.
Say goodbye to all you know,
welcome to the Land of No.

# Der Überhund

Dog hung out in Cat Town,
slept in a bed built for death,
licking the angry red scar
across his heart,
until it was time to act.

Past rats scoffing vomit:
the kings of the bins.
How the dogs had been bought
with the heat from a fire
and a few bones.
Now they wanted their own land
to live out their destiny as dogs.
The future was violence.

Where trees grow through plastic,
lanes lined with the jackal-minded.
Once you loved me son of man,
a snake's love that suppurated.
I licked the sleep from your eyes.
Dead flesh, so fresh
looks so cruelly alive,
soup dripping from your chin,
lying in last night's slops,
gouched out on worms,
running from the past,
running from the pain.
The dog who had sat by his master's grave
went looking for the stars
but they were only sparks.

The rich thick rust of blood,
the metal skank of red,
mouth gagged and legs gaffed,
throat gashed, flies danced.
The groomers and the pimps
haggled over Komondors.
A slaphead flashed the cash,
groped beneath the bitch's legs.
Dogs sitting in piss and shit.
Who will give me fifty for the terrier?
Dog had the man by the throat,
the man held his hand to the hole,
as he choked.
Dog plucked his kidneys from his rib cage,
crunched through fingers
like bread sticks,
chewed off his ears and nose,
nibbled on his toes,
the surloin of the thigh,
the heft of the topside.

We who work for ÜberHund
answer to no one else
and here are the commandments:

      DOG WILL LIV WTH DOG
      MAN IZ AR ENIMEE
      DOG IZ DOGZ BEST FREND
      A DOG SHUD NOT FITE
      WTH ANUTHR DOG
      UNLESS THAT DOG AKTS
      A GAINST HIS NAYTOOR
      ███████████████
      ████████████████

[TEXT REDACTED]

We've just saved your arse, bitch –
we don't want a bleeding medal,
just a bit of light relief
in the house of Der ÜberHund
with Big Billy Big Dick,
the Cock of the North.

DNA does not control behaviour,
it specifies the structure of proteins
and other constitute cells.
A tiny change in DNA can lead
to a huge change in behaviour.
I refer you to the study of the ape,
chimps and bonobos share 99.6 per cent.
They couldn't be more different,
chimps are omnivores,
hunting other kinds of monkeys,
social groups based on coalitions,
highly aggressive to outsiders.
Bonobos are herbivores,
centred round groups of related females,
never known to stoop to murder.
Take the grey wolf, mother of all dogs,
dogs are not pack animals,
dogs are promiscuous, wolves monogamous,
dogs are affable, wolves suspicious of strangers.

Two huge black Cane Corsos
flank the doors of the entrance.
Above the mantel in six-foot letters:

> DOG IS DEAD
> LONG LIVE DER ÜBERHUND

His chest was bare of fur and cloth,
his flesh was ripped with pecs and recs,
arms inked with occult symbols,
wearing black leather trousers
and biker boots,
head sniped like a jackal's,
his fur was golden brown,
eyes as black as hell,
he supped claret from a silver chalice.

Man must be held to account,
must suffer for his sins.
I'm overdue a sermon
and my dogs are getting restless.
I will promise them the earth
free of the middleman
who sits betwixt dogs and gods
above the beast
beneath Der ÜberHund.

## Dog's Final Testament

I                          KAN

NOT

                                      FIX

THE       BLAK

      HOLE

IN       YURE

     SOUL

BY                         FETCHIN

          BALL

YURE            ON

YURE    OWN

NOW

        PAL

# Notes

## The Hand That Cradles the Rock
Gobekli Tepe is a Neolithic archaeological site in South-eastern Anatolia, Turkey. Built and occupied between 9,600 and 7,000 BCE. It marks the transition from hunting and gathering to agriculture, sometimes referred to as the Neolithic Revolution. It was characterised by huge T-shaped pillars. On one of these T-shaped stone pillars, the human arm carved into the vertical stone appears to be holding a dog-like creature, that could be a jackal or some early form of domestic dog.

In 2009 a study looked at ten canid skulls from the Belgian caves of Goyet. One of these skulls was clearly different from the others and was identified as a Paleolithic dog. The Goyet dog originates from 34,000 BCE. Its mitochondrial DNA places it as an ancient sister-group to all modern dogs.

Dmitry Belyayev was a Russian geneticist who was the director of the Institute of Cytology and Genetics. His decades-long effort to breed domesticated silver foxes was described by the *New York Times* as 'arguably the most extraordinary breeding experiment ever conducted.' He has contributed to our understanding of how wolves were domesticated to become dogs.

Lyudmila Trut is a Russian geneticist, ethologist and evolutionist who continued Belyayev's work in Novosibirsk. The experiments began in 1952 and are ongoing. They cover nearly sixty generations of foxes selected for tameness.

Trofim Lysenko was a Soviet agronomist and biologist. He rejected Mendelian genetics in favour of pseudoscientific ideas termed Lysenkoism. 1n 1940 he became director of the Institute of Genetics and used his power to discredit and marginalise his critics. Thousands were incarcerated. Several were sentenced to death, including the botanist Nikolai Vavilov.

## Pekingese

Empress Dowager Cixi (also Tzu-hsi) was a Chinese noble-woman, concubine and regent who controlled the Qing dynasty for 47 years from 1861 until her death in 1908. the Pekingese breed originated in China and could only be owned by members of the Chinese Imperial Palace. They were considered to be sacred Buddhist spirit-animals born from mating a lion with a butterfly. The empress Dowager Cixi was devoted to them and wrote poetry about them. In 1861, during the Opium Wars, captain J. Hart Dunn stole one of the Empress's dogs and gave it to Queen Victoria.

## Turnespete

Turnespete is the name given in *Of English Dogs* (1576) to a short legged, long-bodied dog bred to run on a wheel to turn meat. It is also included in William Bingley's *Memoirs of British Quadrupeds* (1809). It was referred to as a Turnspit Dog, Kitchen Dog, Cooking Dog, and the Underdog. The breed is now extinct. It was bred to run on a wheel so that the meat or fowl would cook evenly. The dogs were also taken to church to serve as foot warmers.

## Chihuahua

'Holy Bonsai Wolf' is a term given to the Chihuahua by David Redmalm, associate professor in Sociology and Social Psychology at Mälardalen University, Sweden. Its ancestor is the Techichi, bred in South America for ritual purposes and food. First by Toltec society and then Aztec. When the Spanish colonized the Mexican region, the Chihuahuas were set free to live in the Mexican mountains.

Bjarne Melgaard is a Norwegian artist based in New York. His first show there featured apes engaging in sexual acts. Another performance involved trained Chihuahuas in various positions to highlight issues of power, socialization and domestication.

Scott Musgrove is an artist who began by depicting extinct animal species. He draws inspiration from Jan Van Eyck and

Hieronymus Bosch to create bizarre and surreal landscapes and animals. One of his paintings features a Chihuahua in a wolf costume.

Daniel Edwards is an American artist whose work addresses celebrity and popular culture. His subjects include Britney Spears, Hillary Clinton and Oprah Winfrey. His sculpture of Prince Harry depicted his corpse in military uniform. His sculpture of a tiara-wearing Paris Hilton on an autopsy slab featured her Chihuahua, Tinkerbell.

In the film *Beverly Hills Chihuahua* (2008), the protagonist Chihuahua, Chloe, is rescued in the deserts of Mexico by hundreds of guerrilla Chihuahuas led by Montezuma, who teaches Chloe about her noble ancestry and explains why they have turned their back on human society.

### Pedomorphosis
Deborah Godwin studied pedomorphosis in dogs, also known as underdevelopment, where adults pass through fewer growth stages and resemble a juvenile stage of its ancestor: a form of arrested development. This is why dogs and especially purebred dogs are less wolf-like than wolves. New-born wolves have small snub noses and floppy ears but the wolf grows up to have a long pointy nose and tall erect ears. Dr Deborah Goodwin and her team found that a dog's facial features correlate with a dog's behaviour. The more a dog resembles a wolf the more it behaves like one. However, the German Shepherd, which was intentionally bred back to look more wolf-like, does not have more wolf-like behaviour. This is probably because once a breed has lost a behaviour it cannot be bred back by a change of appearance.

### Uncle Dolfy's Dog
*Atme tief und ohne angst*, roughly translates as 'breathe deeply and without fear'.

**When the Dogs Found Out What Adolf Learned in Landsberg**
In 1924 Hitler spent 264 days incarcerated in Landsberg prison after being convicted of treason. It was during his imprisonment that he wrote his book *Mein Kampf*. It was also during his time there that he immersed himself in the history of eugenics. One of history's leading eugenicists was an American scientist called Charles Davenport (1866-1944). The Nazis claimed that Davenport and other American eugenicists inspired and supported Hitler's racial purification laws. These same American eugenicists inspired British politician Sewallis Shirley (1844-1904) to form the Kennel Club in 1873, although the selective breeding of dogs is actually a form of dysgenics: the perpetuation of defective and/or disadvantageous genes and traits.

**Underdog and Der Überhund**
In the future, dogs acquire speech. Two opposing underground movements emerge: UnderDog and Der ÜberHund. The first operates through peaceful resistance, acts of nonviolent civil disobedience. The latter is a revolutionary militant group that advocates an 'any means necessary' policy to gain, not just equality, but social and economic power. The leader of this group is a charismatic hybrid of dog and man. He preaches to his dogs and reads from his holy texts, explaining their origins, and their destiny. You have been reading extracts from this tractate. You are now a child of Der ÜberHund.

# Acknowledgments

I am indebted to fellow writers and friends, Claire O'Callaghan, Steve Ely and Jim Greenhalf for their feedback at various stages of the work. I had help with some of the language in the collection from Anne-Laure Corcol (French), Dan McIntyre (Old and Middle English), David Rudrum (German). Thanks to Andy Croft at Smokestack Books for taking a chance with this mongrel text. And to Ted Hughes, for *Crow* which somehow led me to *The Dogs*.

Thank you to Louis Benoit for providing the artwork for this collection. This book is part of a wider 'Dogs' project funded by the Arts Council. Alongside this book, artwork inspired by the poems will be exhibited at various locations. Many thanks to the Arts Council England (and Stephen May in particular) for their help and support.

*'Truth's a dog that must to kennel'*
Shakespeare, *King Lear*